Luke Has Asthma, Too

Alison Rogers

Illustrations by Michael Middleton

Waterfront Books
Burlington, Vermont 05401

To my son, Matthew

Design and production by Robinson Book Associates
Typesetting by PostScript, Inc.
Printed in the United States by Capital City Press

ISBN: 0–914525–06–9
Library of Congress Catalog Card No.: 87–40053

Library of Congress Cataloging-in-Publication Data

Rogers, Alison, 1952–
    Luke has asthma, too.

    1. Asthma in children — Juvenile literature.
I. Middleton, Michael.   II. Title.
RJ436.A8R64   1987   616.92′238   87-40053
ISBN 0–914525–06–9

Foreword

Childhood asthma is a chronic illness that affects 5 percent of the children in the United States. It is frequently undertreated and causes more hospital admissions (140,000 a year), more visits to hospital emergency rooms, and more school absences than any other chronic disease of childhood.

Asthma disrupts the living patterns of children because of its unpredictability. A child may experience an asthma attack suddenly, with little warning, causing upheaval and panic in the family unprepared to deal with it. Parents may worry incessantly—and needlessly—about their child's well-being.

Fortunately, several developments during the past ten years have made asthma more manageable. These include inhaled drugs that are highly effective, longer-lasting medications that have fewer side effects, and preparations that virtually prevent attacks even among children who have chronic asthma. An inexpensive meter has also been developed that measures the peak flow of air from the lung. This device helps parents to predict attacks and to regulate the child's medication. Each of these advances helps many children with asthma. Combined, they are truly powerful.

Most encouraging, the growing interest in self-care among Americans has stimulated parents to play a greater role. A well-informed parent who understands the management of asthma can now make reliable judgments about the child's situation. The parent can control most attacks without panic according to a plan worked out with his or her physician. The child who has moderate asthma can now live a normal life, taking part in all sports and social activities.

This gentle book will make good reading with your child, whether he or she has asthma or not. The story shows that asthma can be managed in a calm fashion. For the more than 2 million families who have children with asthma, this is an important message.

Thomas F. Plaut, M.D., Author of
Children With Asthma: A Manual for Parents

ABOUT THE AUTHOR

Alison Rogers graduated from Harvard University with a Masters degree in Education in Human Development. She is now a doctoral candidate in the same field at the University of Massachusetts at Amherst.

Her professional experience includes work as a mental health consultant, parent educator, teacher trainer, and therapist. She has led support groups for parents of children with asthma.

Ms. Rogers is married to Alan Dayno, M.D. and they have two sons, Matthew, aged six, and Teddy, aged four. Both boys have asthma.

Every day on my way to school, my Mom and I walk past my cousin Luke's house. He is a very big boy. He is nine years old.

Luke goes to school on a yellow bus. He wears a blue backpack and a red baseball cap. Right before he gets on the bus he turns and waves his cap to his Mom.

  The other day I was trying to ride my two wheeler and Luke walked by with his baseball hat on.

  "Hey, Luke," I yelled. I wanted to show him how great I was at riding my bike. I pushed off with my foot. All of a sudden my front wheel wobbled. I fell to the ground.

"Oh, no," I thought. "Luke will really laugh now." But he didn't. Instead he helped me back on my bike.

"Just look straight ahead," he said, "and I will hold your seat."

Together we took off down the street. He let go and I rode a long way by myself. Luke waved his cap to me and ran home.

Someday I will be big like Luke. Then I will be able to do all the things that Luke can do.

I have asthma.

Luke has asthma, too.

When I get a cold and I have asthma, I begin to cough. My chest feels very tight as if the air won't get into my lungs fast enough. Sometimes my stomach hurts, too, and I have to rest.

I have a noisy machine that I breathe from. I call it my pipe. The mist from the machine has medicine in it and makes my chest feel much bigger. Then I can breathe better and play my favorite games.

Luke has a smaller machine called an inhaler that doesn't make noise. He uses it all by himself when his chest feels tight. He carries his in the pouch of his backpack.

In the morning and at night Luke and I take the same medicine. My Mom sprinkles mine in applesauce so I can swallow it more easily. Luke just swallows his with water.

One day after I took my medicine, my asthma did not get better. My Mom and I drove in the car to the hospital emergency room.

The lights were very bright. People were moving around quickly. I sat on a big bed while my Mom talked to the doctor. I felt sick and scared. I heard the doctor say something about needles. I wished I had Pete, my stuffed dog.

Then my mother sat beside me. "You need to stay in the hospital for a few days to get medicine a special way," she said. "The medicine will go in through a vein in your hand. It is called an I.V."

I started to cry and found it hard to breathe. Then I remembered when Luke had to stay in the hospital. He told me about his I.V. He said it only hurt for a few minutes.

A nurse came to get me. She smiled and said, "My name is Ellen. I will take good care of you while you are here." She gave me a puppet and a superhero sticker to wear.

Ellen took me and Mom down the hall to the elevator. We went up to the place where all the kids stay.

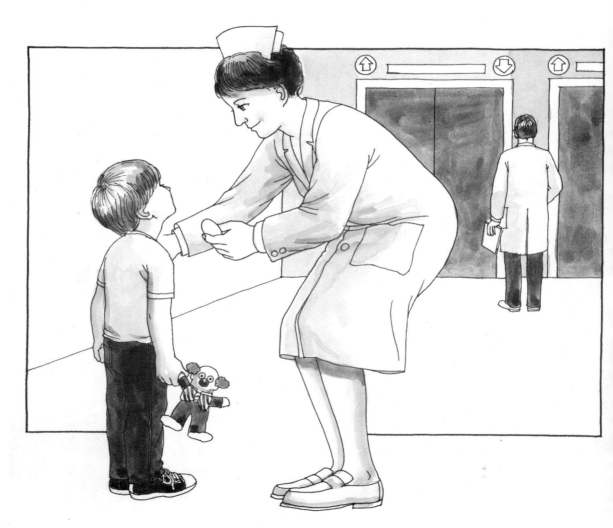

When we got to our room, Mom let me sit on her lap. Ellen got my bed ready and brought me some pajamas with sleeves that tie. I didn't want to put on those silly pajamas. Mom said I had to, but she looked sad.

Ellen told my Mom about other parents who get together to talk. She said they learn all about asthma and about staying healthy, too. That made my Mom look a little happier.

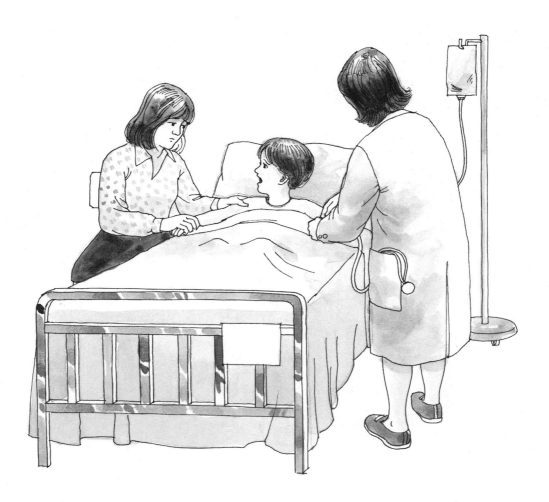

My doctor came in and said it was time to get the special
medicine started. Mom helped me stay still while the doctor put
in the needle. My hand hurt and I started crying again. My
doctor taped up my hand and showed me the bag of medicine
hanging on the pole. The medicine dripped down the tube,
through the needle and into a vein in my hand.

Just then Dad walked into my room. He had Pete, some of my toys from home, and my Superman pajamas. He told me that he would stay with me all night at the hospital. I began to feel better already.

The next morning Dad and I went down the hall to the playroom. Dad pushed the I.V. pole and I walked beside. In the playroom there were fish in a tank, kids watching TV, and games to play.

Dad and I built a hospital with blocks and I got to knock it down. When I looked up I saw a woman come into the room and start talking to all the kids. She said her name was Mrs. Wright.

"I want to show you a special exercise to do when you have trouble breathing," she said. Then she showed us how to sit with our elbows resting on our knees while we leaned forward.

"After you get comfortable, close your eyes and pretend you are floating on a raft in the ocean. Start breathing so you sound like the waves," she explained. She showed us how to breathe in very slowly while she counted to five. As we let our breath out, she counted to five again.

My Dad and I practiced together. Mrs. Wright said we really looked relaxed and sounded like waves.

The next morning I went home. In the car, Dad and I talked about my asthma. He said the doctor told him about many things we can do at home so I probably won't have to go to the hospital again.

I should take my medicine every day. If my chest feels tight, I should tell him and Mom. "Don't worry," I told Dad, "I can help you and Mom take care of me."

We got home and I took off my jacket. Just then the doorbell rang. Mom opened the door and there was Luke with his mother. He was holding something behind his back.

27

He came over to me and put something on my head. It was a red baseball cap just like his. Boy, did I smile hard!

Luke stayed and we rode our bikes together.
It's not fun having asthma, but I always get better.

Resources
for Parents

ORGANIZATIONS

American Lung Association
1740 Broadway
New York, NY 10019

There are more than 300 local and state lung associations across the country. They work to educate the public and health professionals about asthma and other lung diseases. Many lung association chapters have helped parents start support groups. Summer camp programs are also sponsored by local chapters. Your local affiliate should be listed in the white pages under Lung Assocation.

Asthma and Allergy Foundation of America
1717 Massachusetts Ave. N.W.
Suite 305
Washington, DC 20036

A voluntary health organization that provides educational materials for the public and health professionals.

National Jewish Center for Immunology and Respiratory Medicine
1400 Jackson Street
Denver, CO 80206

Engages in treatment, research and education in chronic respiratory diseases. Accepts patients through physician referrals. Provides information on asthma and lung disease via the following toll-free number: 1-800-222-LUNG.

NEWSLETTERS

The MA REPORT
Mothers of Asthmatics, Inc.
5316 Summit Drive
Fairfax, VA 22030

A monthly newsletter directed at parents of children with asthma providing information and support. $10.00 per year.

Asthma Update
123 Monticello Avenue
Annapolis, MD 21401

Quarterly newsletter for parents and patients with asthma. Includes annotated abstracts from current medical literature and perspectives on asthma by health professionals. Four to six pages, $8.00 per year.

BOOKS

Children with Asthma: A Manual for Parents, by Thomas F. Plaut, M.D. 156 pages. Pedipress, Inc., Box 828, Amherst, MA 01004. $9.95 prepaid. This book combines parents' experiences with up-to-date medical information on all aspects of childhood asthma. A pragmatic approach to the difficulties of having a child with asthma, blended with an obvious respect for parents and children. An excellent book.

Teaching Myself About Asthma. by K. Tiernan, P. Nader and L. Weiner. 152 pages. Illustrated. Health Education Associates, 14 North Lake Road, Columbia, SC 29223. $9.95 prepaid. This book helps parents and children who want to understand the nature of asthma to take part in its overall management. Clearly written for children 9 to 12 years of age.

SUPPORT GROUPS

Support Groups for parents of children with asthma, and for children with asthma, can be easily formed in your community with the help of the Respiratory Therapy Department at your hospital, pediatricians, HMOs, and your local chapter of the American Lung Association.

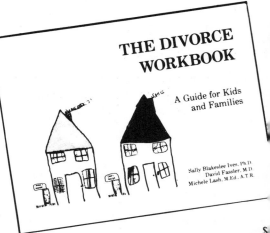